STRANGE
BEAUTY

GERMAN PAINTINGS
AT THE
NATIONAL GALLERY

STRANGE BEAUTY

GERMAN PAINTINGS
AT THE
NATIONAL GALLERY

Caroline Bugler

NATIONAL GALLERY COMPANY, LONDON
DISTRIBUTED BY YALE UNIVERSITY PRESS

First published in Great Britain in 2014 by
National Gallery Company Limited
St Vincent House
30 Orange Street
London WC2H 7HH

www.nationalgallery.org.uk

ISBN: 978 1 85709 570 8
1036268

British Library Cataloguing-in-Publication Data.
A catalogue record is available from the British Library.
Library of Congress Control Number: 2013946858

Publisher Jan Green
Project Editor Giselle Sonnenschein
Picture Researcher Suzanne Bosman
Production Penny Le Tissier and Jane Hyne

Designed by Libanus Press
Printed in the UK by Butler, Tanner & Dennis
Origination by DL Imaging, London

Front cover: Lucas Cranach the Elder, *Cupid Complaining to Venus*, about 1525 (p. 81)
Page 2: Master of the Saint Bartholomew Altarpiece, *Saints Peter and Dorothy*, probably about 1505–10 (detail; p. 58)

All measurements give height before width

National Gallery publications generate valuable revenue for the Gallery,
to ensure that future generations are able to enjoy the paintings as we do today.

CONTENTS

Introduction

The National Gallery's collection of German art includes paintings by some of the world's best-loved artists – Hans Holbein the Younger, Albrecht Dürer, Lucas Cranach the Elder and Caspar David Friedrich – who are all celebrated for their mastery of expression, their inventiveness and their technical skills. Sitting alongside their pictures are many works by less famous German artists, several of them anonymous, which also possess great originality and beauty, and add their own narrative to the story of German art. Their portraits enable us to put a face to rulers, courtiers and traders – even when we do not know the artists' names. Altarpieces and small devotional works reveal a great deal about painters' religious beliefs, while the landscape backgrounds of these pictures give tantalising glimpses of the towns and countryside where they lived, and mythological pictures provide an insight into their imaginative worlds. Defining national characteristics in art is always fraught with difficulty, but if there is a thread that connects these diverse works it is that many of them possess a singular – even strange – beauty, an emotional power, a resonant use of colour and an angularity of form. German artists often reveal an original vision that does not shy away from the darker aspects of the human psyche, the frankly ugly, the grotesque or surreal. An energetic use of line and expressive distortion is also often particularly evident in drawings and prints (figs 1 and 2).

While the Gallery's German paintings collection spans a period of five hundred years, it is strongest in art of the fifteenth and sixteenth centuries – the period when Germany produced the rich crop of outstanding artists who are the main focus of this book. The earliest German works in the collection were made shortly after European art had been revolutionised by the invention of oil paints. Oils gave artists considerable freedom, enabling them to render what they saw or imagined in astonishingly minute detail, and in brilliant jewel-like colours. What is particularly noticeable in these fifteenth-century

Fig. 1 Martin Schongauer, *The Temptation of Saint Anthony*, 1470s
Copperplate engraving, 31.2 x 23 cm, The British Museum, London
Martin Schongauer imaginatively interprets the torments of Saint Anthony in the Egyptian desert, when he was attacked by devils as he levitated in the air.

7

German paintings is how similar they are to Netherlandish works, some of the same period. There were strong connections between the two regions at the time, and artists and images circulated freely between them. Hans Memling, for example, who was born in Germany around 1430, spent his working life in Bruges, and is now thought of as a Flemish artist (fig. 3). The influence of his Netherlandish master Rogier van der Weyden (1399/1400–1464), famous for the naturalism of his details and the expressive pathos of his figures, was widely felt in Germany, communicated through prints and by the presence of his majestic

Fig. 2 Matthias Grünewald, *An Elderly Woman with Clasped Hands*, about 1520
Charcoal or black chalk on paper, 38 x 24 cm, Ashmolean Museum, Oxford

Grünewald's sensitive drawing of an elderly woman with hands clasped in prayer encapsulates the expressive power of his art.

Fig. 3 Hans Memling, *The Virgin and Child with an Angel*, about 1480
Oil on oak, 54.2 x 37.4 cm

This small altarpiece was painted for private devotion, and features an unidentified donor, who commissioned the painting, kneeling before the Virgin and Child.

Columba altarpiece (about 1455) in the church of St Columba in Cologne. The influence did not just flow one way: Rogier himself adopted some motifs and ideas from German artists working in Cologne.

Germany did not exist as a unified nation when the paintings in this book were created. From 962 until 1806, a confederation of German-speaking states (at one time as many as 300) in central and northern Europe were loosely bound together under the rulership of a Holy Roman Emperor, chosen by seven 'Electors' from different states. Territorial boundaries shifted over time, but around 1500 this empire encompassed present-day Germany, Austria, Alsace, much of Switzerland, the Czech Republic, Slovenia and parts of northern Italy. Because of this geographical spread it is hard to separate the historic art of Germany from that of neighbouring countries, particularly Austria and Switzerland. The position of the German lands in the centre of Europe also made them a crossroads for artistic ideas. The emperors Rudolph II and Maximilian had strong and influential artistic tastes, but a variety of attitudes and outlooks coexisted. Individual cities – including Nuremberg, Colmar, Cologne, Augsburg, Mainz, Strasbourg, Basel, Vienna and Prague – developed into flourishing independent hubs of creative production, supported by the patronage of local princes, merchants and religious institutions (fig. 4).

Art was a luxury denoting wealth, status and scholarship, and in the early sixteenth century rulers of European courts, who were caught up in political rivalry, competed to attract the most illustrious painters, sculptors and craftsmen. Artists were expected to promote princely prestige not only through portraiture, but also by providing designs for pageants, masquerades and tournaments. Civic dignitaries and wealthy traders were also keen to secure the services of the best artists they could afford to capture their likenesses in portraits or to paint lavish altarpieces that would help ensure their immortality. German artists travelled from city to city in their search for training and commissions. Dürer, who was born in Nuremberg in 1471, journeyed to Colmar (intending to visit the artist Martin Schongauer), Basel and Strasbourg; Venice, Bologna and Rome (where he encountered Italian art at first hand); and Antwerp, Brussels, Mechelen and Aachen. Holbein, who was born in Augsburg in 1497, began his career in Basel, visited Paris and had two prolonged stays in England in 1526–8 and 1532–43, becoming court painter to the English King Henry VIII. There is no record of Holbein visiting Italy, but he certainly knew of compositions by Mantegna and other north Italian artists, which he probably studied in prints.

For if artists travelled, so too did the images they created. Ideas could circulate

with remarkable rapidity in Renaissance Europe thanks to printing. Following Johann Gutenberg's invention of movable metal type in the mid-fifteenth century, printed books were distributed throughout Europe. The thoughts of scholars and theologians such as Erasmus and Martin Luther could now be spread through the printed word – with far-reaching consequences. Illuminated manuscripts had always been a luxury for the few, but printed books illustrated with woodcuts, and later with the more sophisticated copper engravings, could be bought by a wider range of people. Prints were also sold as images independent of book illustration. Dürer found a ready market for his woodcuts and engravings, even employing an agent to sell them (fig. 5).

If the first half of the sixteenth century – the age of Dürer and Holbein – represented a highpoint in German painting, the works produced in the decades following their deaths were less remarkable. It was not until the end of the sixteenth century that a fresh influx of ideas injected new life into German art. Bartholomeus Spranger and Hans von Aachen both ventured south of the Alps, where they encountered the Italian Mannerist style at its source. The courts of Munich, Vienna, Innsbruck and Prague also attracted Flemish and Italian artists, fostering an outlook that was truly international. Two prominent German artists of the early seventeenth century, Adam Elsheimer and Johann Liss, even spent most of their careers in Italy.

However, the Thirty Years War (1618–1648), partly ignited by religious conflict in the wake of the Reformation, had a devastating effect on the population of the German lands. The economy was badly damaged, and German art was effectively polarised into north and south. The Protestant princes of the northern states turned their eyes towards the Netherlands, where the realism of the Italian artist Caravaggio and his followers had been imported and interpreted by Dutch and Flemish painters. In the eighteenth century some north German artists even consciously emulated the art of the Low Countries, creating paintings that could pass for works by Dutch masters such as Cuyp or Ostade (fig. 6). The Catholic south was more receptive to the flamboyance of Italian Baroque painting. Monasteries, palaces and churches were covered with exuberant scenes that revealed a desire to match the grand decorative schemes of Rome. As the Baroque style merged into

Fig. 4 Stephan Lochner, *Three Saints*, about 1450
Oil on oak, 68.6 x 59.9 cm

Stephan Lochner was the most important artist working in Cologne in the mid-fifteenth century, and painted several altarpieces in a soft late Gothic style for the city's churches.

Fig. 5 Albrecht Dürer, *Adam and Eve,* 1504
Engraving, 25.2 x 19.3 cm, The British Museum, London

One of Dürer's best known prints, this shows the artist's fascination with human form and his obsession with proportion. The male nude resembles the Hellenistic sculpture of the Apollo Belvedere, excavated in Italy in 1504.

the lighter Rococo, Italian artists and craftsmen working in Germany provided inspiration to local artists. The ambitious frescoes created by Giambattista Tiepolo in the eighteenth century, for example, were to have a profound effect on German painters such as Franz Anton Maulbertsch, who created decorative and lively allegories for the new churches and palaces that were springing up in a great outburst of building activity.

The early nineteenth century saw a reaction against such dazzling complexity. A band of earnest young artists in Vienna, later dubbed 'the Nazarenes', set up a fraternity and moved to Rome in 1810. Repudiating what they saw as the superficiality and virtuosity of the Baroque and Rococo, they looked to the art of the Middle Ages and Renaissance in their search for a more simple and honest approach. The Nazarenes were particularly drawn to spiritual subjects – as were a group of artists in northern Germany led by Caspar David Friedrich. But for these painters it was the German landscape that provided the potential for spiritual renewal. Infused with a Romantic sense of divinity in nature, Friedrich's paintings feature recognisably northern motifs: Gothic cathedrals and mountain peaks swathed in mist, seascapes, crosses, cliffs, fir trees and lonely figures, often viewed from behind. Some commentators have seen in them a reflection of an embryonic German nation struggling to form a language to express its identity. That identity coalesced with the German unification that took place in 1871, when the career of Adolph von Menzel –

much admired by both the German Kaiser and Otto von Bismarck – was at its height. Menzel was a devoted chronicler of episodes from German history and the heroism of contemporary life. It would be up to a future generation of German artists – the Expressionists – to examine the state of the human soul in the modern Germany that was being created.

Fig. 6 Heinrich Wilhelm Schweickhardt, *Cattle*, 1794
Oil on mahogany, 46.4 x 61 cm

At first glance this painting looks like one of the cattle scenes painted by the seventeenth-century Dutch artist Aelbert Cuyp, though Schweickhardt was actually born in Germany.

THE HUMAN IMAGE

Artists have always played an important role in promoting the status and image of rulers and nobles, and in the German lands from the Renaissance period onwards they were also called upon to capture the likenesses of increasingly confident wealthy bankers and businessmen, especially those who lived in the northern cities of the Hanseatic League. Patrons who were rich and pious enough to commission altarpieces for religious institutions often had themselves and their families included in 'donor portraits', kneeling in prayer below or to one side of the central image, helping to perpetuate their social standing and to solicit prayers for their souls after their deaths.

Centuries before the invention of photography, painted portraits played a central role in diplomatic and marriage negotiations. The English King Henry VIII had to rely on his court artist Holbein to capture the likeness of the Duchess of Milan when he was considering her as a prospective marriage partner, and for that he wanted a painting that conveyed a reasonably realistic idea of her appearance. Holbein took the art of naturalistic portraiture to new heights, and the many detailed drawings he made in preparation for his paintings show the immense care he took to faithfully note down individual characteristics. Indeed, Holbein's portraits of the personalities of Henry's court are so vivid and believable that they define our visual image of the period.

Portraits were commissioned for a number of other reasons too. They might commemorate appointment to public office, be given as gifts to friends, be painted in pairs to mark a betrothal or friendship, or, as Dürer put it, simply 'preserve the look of people after their deaths'. In addition to the carefully rendered details of costume, accessories and decoration that spelled out a sitter's status or occupation, portraitists almost always included some clue as to the painting's purpose, whether it was a flower that hinted at love or commemoration or the paraphernalia of books and writing equipment that surrounded a writer. But what most of the portraits in this chapter share is a directness that conveys a forceful sense of personality. Many of them show the sitter turned towards the left or right rather than facing the viewer, which adds to their sense of animation. The majority do not conform to an ideal standard of beauty, but are firmly grounded in the naturalistic preferences of northern European art.

Master of the Mornauer Portrait, *Portrait of Alexander Mornauer*

about 1464–88, oil on wood, 45.2 x 38.7 cm

The inscription on the piece of paper this man holds in his right hand identifies him as Alexander Mornauer, Town Clerk of Landshut in Bavaria. But for much of the portrait's existence he was described as the great Protestant reformer Martin Luther, and the painting was ascribed to Holbein. When the National Gallery acquired it in 1990 it had the type of deep blue background seen in many Holbein portraits (see page 28), but scientific investigation revealed that the blue paint had been added sometime in the eighteenth century (when the shape of the hat was also altered), presumably so the portrait could be passed off as a work by the great German master. The Gallery removed these later additions, exposing the original wood grain background underneath. The portrait may have been stripped of its glamorous associations, but the presence of the man is conveyed with a striking directness.

Swabian School,
Portrait of a Woman of the Hofer Family

about 1470, oil on silver fir,
53.7 x 40.8 cm

We do not know much about the sitter beyond what the inscription in the top left-hand corner tells us – that she was born into the Hofer family (the surname is a common one in southern Germany). She is holding a forget-me-not in her left hand, perhaps inviting the viewer to remember her during her lifetime or after her death. The flower is also associated with love in German poetry, so the portrait might commemorate a betrothal. Our eyes are almost irresistibly drawn to the fly on the elaborate headdress. By painting minutely detailed insects like this artists could show off their skills in illusionistic portrayal. At the same time, since the fly carries disease and is a symbol of evil or sin, it could evoke thoughts of mortality and serve as a talisman against malevolence or illness.

After Albrecht Dürer,
The Painter's Father

1497, oil on lime, 51 x 40.3 cm

In 1636 the city of Nuremberg presented
two paintings to the English King Charles I.
They were described as a self portrait by Dürer
and a portrait by Dürer of his father. The
self portrait has been identified as an authentic
work, now in the Prado, Madrid, but the
authorship of the National Gallery's painting
has long been debated. Although it is the
best of the four known portraits of the elder
Dürer, its quality and technique do not match
other works by the artist. The faded pink
background is not seen in any of his other
pictures, and the cracked surface, produced
by applying paint quickly in a single layer, is
untypical. It is most likely that this is a copy of
a lost Dürer original, made in the second half
of the sixteenth century, when copies of the
artist's work began to be produced.

Lucas Cranach the Elder, *Portrait of Johann the Steadfast*

1509, oil on wood,
41.2 x 31 cm

Lucas Cranach the Elder, *Portrait of Johann Friedrich the Magnanimous*

1509, oil on wood,
41.9 x 31.5 cm

1509

The portrait of Cranach's patron the Elector of Saxony (1468–1532) is joined as a diptych with that of his six-year-old son, Johann Friedrich the Magnanimous, who succeeded him as elector in 1532. The two portraits are closely related in their colour scheme, the green background of the father's portrait echoed in the green clothing of the son. Diptych portraits usually show married couples rather than fathers and sons, and this pairing may have arisen because Johann Friedrich's mother had died giving birth to him. Both sitters are splendidly attired, their costumes adorned with expensive jewels. The young boy's hat is surmounted by multicoloured ostrich plumes, which were fashionable at courts in northern Europe at the time. But there is a sense of immediacy and expressiveness about the portrait that allows us to see the child beneath the finery.

Hans Baldung Grien,
Portrait of a Man

1514, oil on lime,
59.3 x 48.9 cm

We do not know the precise identity of this handsomely dressed sitter with grey eyes and flowing locks and beard, but his clothing and accessories offer some clues. He is obviously a man of some wealth; his black hat is adorned with a small gold brooch and under his fur-lined coat he wears two gold chains, one of which supports two badges. The first shows the Virgin and Child, the insignia of the Order of Our Lady of the Swan, whose members were of noble birth. The second denotes the knightly Swabian Fish and Falcon jousting company. When the National Gallery acquired the painting in the mid-nineteenth century it was thought to be by Dürer, but a false Dürer monogram was removed in 1957.

Lucas Cranach the Elder, *Portrait of a Woman*

1525–7, oil on wood, 36.1 x 25.1 cm

While this is usually described as a portrait, it may just be an idealised image of a beautiful, richly dressed woman rather than a specific individual. But the letter 'M' embroidered on her bodice could provide a clue to her identity. With her elaborate cloth of gold costume, pearls, gold jewellery and bold frontal gaze the lady has an air of languid seduction.

Hans Holbein the Younger, *Erasmus*

1523, oil on wood, 73.6 x 51.4 cm,
On loan from Longford Castle collection

The Dutch humanist and theologian Erasmus (1466/9–1536) was one of the most famous writers of his day and a great friend of Holbein, who painted his portrait on a number of occasions. Erasmus needed several portraits to send to his many friends and admirers in Europe, and this one went to William Warham, Archbishop of Canterbury. It shows Erasmus in his early fifties, surrounded by items which reflect his scholarly interests. His hands rest on a book whose pages bear a Greek inscription referring to the Labours of Hercules – probably a humorous allusion to the painstakingly detailed commentaries that Erasmus supplied with his Latin translation of the New Testament. A Latin couplet on the book on the back shelf, perhaps by Erasmus himself, praises Holbein's skill: 'I am Johannes (i.e. Hans) Holbein, whom it is easier to denigrate than to emulate.'

Hans Holbein the Younger, *Lady with a Squirrel and a Starling*

about 1526–8, oil on oak, 56 x 38.8 cm

Holbein's lady holds her pet squirrel by a chain, while a starling, which might also be a pet, perches in a branch beside her ear. She is thought to be Anne Lovell, and both creatures probably allude to her family name. Similar squirrels were shown on the coat of arms of the Lovell family, and the Lovells lived at East Harling in Norfolk. The painting is an outstanding example of how skilled Holbein was at rendering texture. The squirrel's gleaming eye contrasts with the soft white ermine of the headdress, which itself invites comparison with the crisp border of the shawl and the transparent chemise. The sitter seems slightly detached from her environment, gazing out beyond the picture rather than focusing on the pet she holds. This could be because the picture was composed in stages rather than all at once, and the squirrel was a later addition.

Hans Holbein the Younger, *Christina of Denmark, Duchess of Milan*

1538, oil on oak, 179.1 x 82.6 cm

In 1538, when Henry VIII was considering marrying the young Christina, Duchess of Milan, he sent Holbein to Brussels to capture her likeness. The sitting lasted three hours, and the image Holbein showed Henry on his return – probably an initial drawing for this portrait – certainly pleased the King. The imperial ambassador reported that 'since he saw it he has been in much better humor than he ever was, making his musicians play on their instruments all day long'. The finished painting shows the 16-year-old duchess, who was already a widow, in mourning dress. Her face and elegant hands are clearly presented against her dark costume. Despite the favourable impression given by the painting, marriage negotiations were abandoned due to political circumstances.

South German School, *Portrait of a Man*

about 1530–40, oil on beech, 49.9 x 39.1 cm

This unidentified young man with clear blue eyes and corkscrew curls is holding two red carnations or pinks. The flower was associated with Christ's Passion, as well as with betrothal in German portraiture, where it is sometimes worn in bridal wreaths. The portrait is one of a pair probably showing a bridal couple; the woman's portrait in the Oskar Reinhart collection in Winterthur shows her holding a lily, which was also associated with marriage. The young man's fine clothes with luxurious touches indicate high social standing.

HOLBEIN'S AMBASSADORS

This painting is a record of a friendship between two men – Jean de Dinteville (1504–1555), the French ambassador to London, and Georges de Selve (1508/9–1541), Bishop of Lavaur in south-west France, on a secret mission to the English court – and the moment when they met in London. Holbein painted it in 1533, the year after he arrived in London for his second stay – he was to remain in the city until his death in 1543. He signed the work prominently in the left-hand corner. An unusual masterpiece, which shows the artist at the height of his powers, it was probably the work by which he would most have liked to be remembered.

It is unusual in showing two sitters who are not related; the format of two full-length figures standing side-by-side belongs to the German tradition of portraits of rulers or married or betrothed couples. Dinteville (left) wears a splendid pink satin doublet and black fur-trimmed cloak. His companion (p. 34) is more soberly dressed, as befits a cleric, but his brown damask robe would have been an expensive luxury. The two men are standing in front of a green damask curtain and on a floor inlaid with marble. The objects on the shelves are not necessarily ones owned by the sitters; they have all been chosen for their symbolic significance. The most puzzling item in the picture is the grey shape – a distorted skull – that cuts across the foreground.

The French King Francis I had sent Dinteville to England to report on what was happening at the English court during a pivotal political moment. Henry VIII was divorcing his wife Catherine of Aragon so he could marry Anne Boleyn, and in order to do so had bypassed papal authority and established the Church of England as a separate institution from that of Rome. It looked as though the way might be open for Protestantism to flourish in England, which could potentially lead to the destabilising of good relations between England and France. Dinteville complained that he was 'the most melancholy, weary and wearisome ambassador that ever was seen'. He had only planned to stay in London for six months, but Anne Boleyn's pregnancy and coronation meant that he had to prolong his visit to witness the arrival of the new child to which the French king was to be godfather. Whatever else Dinteville's diplomatic mission may have achieved, the double portrait he commissioned was its most triumphant outcome. He took it back to his chateau in France when he returned in the autumn of 1533.

The 25-year-old Georges de Selve was already an accomplished ambassador when Holbein captured his likeness during his visit to his unhappy friend in London. He had been made a bishop while still in his teens, and in 1529 had attended the Diet of Speyer, when the Holy Roman Emperor Charles V attempted to reconcile the Catholics and Protestants in Germany. De Selve's hopes for Christian unity were never realised, and he died in 1541, aged 32.

Hans Holbein the Younger, *The Ambassadors*

1533, oil on oak, 207 x 209.5 cm

The arithmetic book, which is one that was published in 1527, is open at a page that begins with the word 'Divide' – an appropriate enough word for two ambassadors who were trying to promote unity.

The Lutheran hymnal was published in Wittenberg in 1524, and the two hymns shown are *Veni Sancte Spiritus* (Come Holy Spirit) and the *Ten Commandments*. The inclusion of a Lutheran text in German in a portrait of two Catholics might seem unusual, but the texts were of universal Christian significance, and it may be that Georges de Selve wanted them shown to reinforce his wish for Christian unity. Musical instruments were often used to signify harmony, lack of harmony being a metaphor for worldly conflict. The broken string on the lute could signify the discord in a troubled Europe that both ambassadors were trying to remedy, while the music of flutes was more traditionally associated with war than with gentlemanly music-making. The compass underneath the lute is a traditional attribute of the planet Saturn, and linked with Melancholy in a famous woodcut by Dürer – and perhaps also by association with Dinteville's frame of mind.

The objects on the top shelf include a celestial globe and instruments such as quadrants and dials, which depend on the sun for telling the time, measuring altitudes and finding the positions of celestial bodies. But the instruments are not set to record the exact date or the place where the portrait was painted – Holbein could have based them on sketches he had made of instruments for other pictures. It is difficult to interpret the meaning behind the objects, but they may simply represent the passing of time.

On the bottom shelf is a terrestrial globe including the word 'Polisy' – the name of the Dinteville family chateau, where the painting was originally displayed. The globe shows the New World and the line established by the Pope at the Treaty of Tordesillas in 1494, which divided Spanish and Portuguese colonial possessions.

The crucifix just glimpsed behind the curtain in the top left corner provides a counterpart to the skull, alluding to the hope of salvation after death through faith.

Skulls often appear in sixteenth- and seventeenth-century paintings to suggest mortality, and that meaning must apply here. Dinteville, who was miserable and ill in England, may well have found his thoughts turning to death and redemption. He even sports a badge of a skull on his hat – though skull jewellery was not uncommon at the time. The skull is subject to a type of distortion known as anamorphosis. When the finished picture is viewed from a specific angle on the right-hand side of the painting the distortion is corrected (see right).

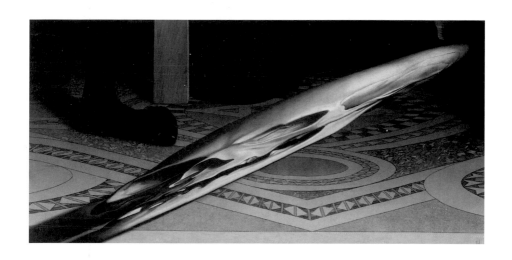

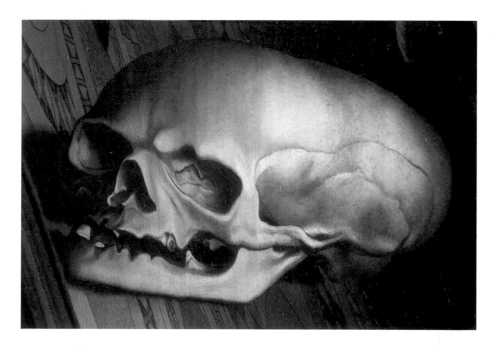

The pattern on the inlaid marble floor resembles one in Westminster Abbey sanctuary. The Abbey's floor was designed to represent the cosmos, and it may be that Holbein meant his floor to have the same symbolic connotation.

Holbein was enormously skilled at capturing surface details. Close inspection of Dinteville's right hand holding its dagger reveals the contrasting textures of soft flesh, silky fur, crisp linen, the dull gleam of metalwork and the subtle glint of gold threads. An embossed inscription on the dagger reveals that Dinteville was 29 years old.

Hans Holbein the Younger, *William Reskimer*

about 1532–4, black and coloured chalks, pen and ink, and metalpoint on paper, 29.0 x 21.0 cm,
Royal Collection Trust, London

It is highly unlikely that Holbein made his sitters pose side-by-side for hours in the room
while he painted them. He generally made detailed preparatory sketches for his portraits,
drawing his sitters from life, and using the drawings to work up finished paintings without
the sitter needing to be present. No such drawings survive for *The Ambassadors*, but he
would no doubt have followed this procedure when composing the picture. This drawing
of William Reskimer, made in the same year he painted *The Ambassadors*, shows the
level of detail that he included in his initial drawings. In the case of a large painting like
The Ambassadors, he may have assembled several smaller studies to make one large cartoon
of the whole, allowing him to move the component parts around to make adjustments to
the composition.

Reskemeer a Cornish   Gent:

45

EXPRESSING THE SACRED

In the fifteenth century artists found their main source of employment in producing devotional images. Nowhere was this more true than in the populous and wealthy city of Cologne, a major pilgrimage centre that had so many churches it was described as the 'German Rome'. Altarpieces were often complex works consisting of several panels, but many have been dismantled, so several of the religious works on the Gallery's walls are fragments of a much larger whole. Painted and sculpted altarpieces were produced to commission, but prints could be run off speculatively, and religious engravings, especially suitable as aids to private worship, allowed imagery to circulate rapidly. One of the most famous series of prints – Dürer's *Apocalypse* of 1498 – contains frightening imagery of the Last Judgement, which must have seemed terrifyingly close, since many people believed the world would end in 1500.

In an uncertain universe, the Church may have provided comfort and hope, but the institution itself was in turmoil. In 1517, Martin Luther nailed his *Ninety-five Theses* to the door of Wittenberg Castle Church, condemning corruption in the Catholic Church, specifically the sale of indulgences (reductions to the time a sinner would be punished, either in life or in Purgatory). He was giving voice to a longstanding and widespread desire for church reform that ultimately led to a schism in Western Christianity, and the establishment of Protestantism. Artists were intimately involved in the religious debates. Luther's friend Cranach found patronage in Wittenberg and began to develop a form of art that satisfied Lutheran liturgy. Dürer was part of a scholarly circle in Nuremberg that discussed and supported the movement for reform, and he followed Luther's career with enthusiasm. But the Reformation had negative consequences for some: in Strasbourg and Basel paintings were destroyed, and many artists lost their livelihood.

At the end of the sixteenth century, the ecclesiastical reforms instigated by the Catholic Church in response to the Reformation restored Catholicism's self-confidence, and created a steadier demand for religious works. The paintings of Rottenhammer, Spranger, Elsheimer and Liss reflect a new energy in religious art, which looked to Italy for inspiration.

The Master of Saint Veronica, *Saint Veronica with the Sudarium*

about 1420, oil on walnut, 44.2 x 33.7 cm

According to a medieval legend, Saint Veronica wiped Christ's face with her handkerchief as he carried his Cross towards Calvary, and as a reward for her compassion his features were miraculously imprinted on the cloth (the sudarium). Here she holds up the cloth to the viewer, casting her eyes down towards the miraculous image in a mood of devotional contemplation that it would have been intended to invoke in the beholder. Her hands and halo appear to overlap the picture's border, giving the illusion that they are projecting into the viewer's space, and Christ's head seems to hover above the cloth rather than be imprinted on it, adding to the sense of holy presence. Little is known about the Master of Saint Veronica other than that he or she worked in Cologne in the early years of the fifteenth century.

Master of the Life of the Virgin,
The Presentation in the Temple

probably about 1460–75, oil on oak, 83.8 x 108.6 cm

The Virgin presents her son to a priest, forty days after his birth, as required by Jewish law. Saint Joseph reaches into his pocket to give the customary gift of money, and behind him a woman carries the traditional offering of two doves. The setting is contemporary Europe, and the priest wears the garments of a Christian cleric. A carved altarpiece behind him depicts scenes from the Old Testament which prefigure Christ's sacrifice. The angular figures and drapery indicate that the anonymous artist knew the work of Flemish masters such as Rogier van der Weyden, and that he may have been trained in the Netherlands. The gold background and shallow space give the work a distinctly medieval feel. This is one of eight panels showing episodes from the life of the Virgin painted for the church of Saint Ursula in Cologne (the other seven are in the Alte Pinakothek, Munich).

Master of the Aachen Altarpiece, *The Crucifixion*

1490–5, oil on oak, 107.3 x 120.3 cm,
Left- and right-hand panels: The Walker Art Gallery, Liverpool

This triptych, which tells the story of Christ's Passion, was
commissioned for a church in Cologne. The narrative begins
on the left-hand shutter, which shows Christ before Pilate,
and continues through the central scene, which is dominated
by the large Crucifixion with vignettes of Christ carrying the
Cross and being taken down from it after his death in the
background, and finishes with the Lamentation scene on the
right shutter. Christ's comparative serenity presents a contrast
with the contorted forms of the two thieves, whose legs have
been broken, and the grotesque faces of his tormentors.
Richly patterned, luxurious fabrics contrast with more
mundane details such as the veins in the leg of the man in
the foreground, plants sprouting from the stony ground,
and the toad by the skull.

Master of the Saint Bartholomew Altarpiece, *The Deposition*

about 1500–5, oil on oak, 74.9 x 47.3 cm

In this richly expressive work Christ is taken down from the cross. His rigid body is supported by the elderly Joseph of Arimathea, who arranged for his burial, the Pharisee Nicodemus in a fur-lined cloak, and a young boy in an improbably athletic pose at the top of the composition. Tears course down the faces of the mourners – the three Holy Women, the swooning Virgin and Saint John the Evangelist – and Saint John's toes even seem to curl up in anguish. The episode is set against the shallow space of a golden sculpted shrine, yet the figures spill out into a naturalistic rocky foreground on which a skull, which marks out the place as Golgotha ('the place of the skull'), and the pot of ointment with which Mary Magdalene anointed Christ, are prominently displayed.

Master of the Saint Bartholomew Altarpiece, *Saints Peter and Dorothy*

probably 1505–10, oil on oak, 125.7 x 71.1 cm

Saints Peter and Dorothy stand against a richly patterned gold damask cloth, beyond which can be glimpsed distant hills; it is as though the gold background of the medieval altarpiece is giving way to the landscape typically seen in Renaissance religious paintings. Peter holds the keys to heaven and hell, and also carries a book covered with soft leather and a pair of glasses to help him read. Dorothy carries a basket of pink and white roses, violets and cornflowers, and wears a garland of similar flowers. According to legend she promised an unbeliever that he would receive flowers and fruit from her when she had passed into paradise. This panel would once have been a shutter for a larger altarpiece; a related one, showing Saint Andrew and Saint Columba, is in the Landesmuseum, Mainz, but a central panel has not been identified.

Master of Cappenberg (Jan Baegert?), *Christ before Pilate*

about 1520, oil on oak, 99.1 x 69.2 cm

Towards the end of the fifteenth century the so-called Master of Liesborn began a large winged altarpiece for the high altar of the Benedictine Abbey of Liesborn in Westphalia. There are eight surviving fragments in the Gallery's collection, of which this is one. It is part of the shutters, and was painted by a later artist, thought to be Jan Baegert, who completed the altarpiece. In this panel, Pilate is washing his hands of the deed after he has been persuaded to have Christ crucified. The woman standing behind him is his wife, who dreamed that Christ was innocent and should be spared death. The subject may be harrowing, but the painting is full of decorative and beguiling details, such as the striped hose of the soldier on the right and the white dog moving forward towards Christ, which is based on an engraving of the same subject by Martin Schongauer.

Lucas Cranach the Elder, *Saints Genevieve and Apollonia, Christina and Ottilia*

1506, oil on lime, 123.5 x 66.4 cm, 121.5 x 63.8 cm

These two panels showing female saints formed the outer faces of the shutters of Cranach's 'Saint Catherine Altarpiece', the rest of which is in the Gemäldegalerie, Dresden. Saint Genevieve, patron saint of Paris, holds the candle that miraculously relit after it was extinguished, and Saint Apollonia of Alexandria carries a pair of pincers, which refer to her torture by having her teeth extracted. Saint Christina stands on a millstone to which she was tied and thrown into the Lake of Bolsena, but she miraculously survived because the stone floated. Her companion, Saint Ottilia, patron saint of Alsace, holds a book on which she displays a pair of eyeballs – a reference to her blindness, which was miraculously cured at her baptism. She wears the black habit of a Benedictine abbess.

Hans Baldung Grien, *The Trinity and Mystic Pietà*

1512, oil on oak, 112.3 x 89.1 cm

Hans Baldung Grien worked with Dürer in Nuremberg, although he was born and settled in Strasbourg. This painting was probably made for the Church of Saint Pierre-le-Vieux in the city. The body of Christ is supported in the dark red marbled stone tomb by God the Father, the Virgin and Saint John the Evangelist. Above them the dove of the Holy Spirit breaks through the grey clouds. The small figures kneeling on the grass below the tomb are probably the donors who commissioned the painting; the coat of arms on the bottom left may be that of the Bettschold family of Strasbourg and the arms on the bottom right are possibly those of the Rothschild family. The central male figure, dressed as a canon, raises his hand as if to greet or intercede with Christ, while the other figures join their hands in prayer. The artist invites the viewer to share the grief of death, just as Christ's heavenly father and earthly mother mourn as parents.

Johann Rottenhammer, *The Coronation of the Virgin*

probably 1596–1606, oil on copper, 92.7 x 63.5 cm

Rottenhammer, who worked in Italy at the turn of the seventeenth century, shows the Virgin, borne aloft by angels, being crowned by God the Father and Jesus while the dove of the Holy Spirit radiates light from above. Saint John the Baptist, clad in red, kneels to the right of the Virgin and Adam and Eve appear just below her. On their left are Saint Peter, Abraham, Isaac and David. On their right are Jonah leaning over the whale which swallowed him; Moses with his stone tablets; and Saint Paul. In the lower part of the picture the saintly assembly includes the Four Fathers of the Church (Jerome, Augustine, Gregory and Ambrose); the female saints Justina, Lucy and Catherine of Alexandria; the Four Evangelists (Luke, John, Mark and Matthew) as well as Saints Francis and Lawrence. Cardinal Camillo Borghese, who commissioned the painting, is evidently the bearded figure looking out towards the viewer.

Bartholomeus
Spranger,
*The Adoration
of the Kings*

about 1595, oil on canvas,
199.8 x 143.7 cm

Spranger was court painter to the Holy Roman Emperor Rudolf II, and his canvases blend the
realistic traditions of Netherlandish painting with the sophisticated Mannerist style he learnt
in Italy. Here, three splendidly dressed kings present their gifts to the Virgin and Child. The
setting is particularly elaborate, and the viewer's eye is invited to roam through complicated
architectural details, arches and ruins. The scene is set at night, giving plenty of opportunity
for dramatic tonal contrasts as brilliant acid colours are highlighted against deep shadows.

Adam Elsheimer,
The Baptism of Christ

about 1599, oil on copper,
28.1 x 21 cm

Christ is being baptised by Saint John in the River Jordan as angels descend bearing a red cloak to cover him. God the Father sits above in the clouds as the Holy Spirit in the form of a dove descends in a blaze of light. The large shadowy figure in the foreground pulling off his shoe may still be in an unbaptised heathen state. Plenty of other details gradually reveal themeselves: figures wearing exotic headgear pointing towards the main scene, a black boy, a woman nursing a baby, and in the distance a boat coming in to shore and a man ploughing with a horse. Elsheimer probably painted this panel when he was working in Venice; it certainly shows the influence of dramatic compositions by the Venetian artists Veronese and Tintoretto that were on display in the city.

Johann Liss, *Judith in the Tent of Holofernes*

about 1622, oil on canvas, 128.5 x 99 cm

The Apocryphal Book of Judith tells the story of an Old Testament heroine who helped the Jews in their struggle against oppression. When the Israelite city of Bethulia was under siege by the Assyrians, Judith gained entry to the camp of the enemy commander Holofernes and, following a banquet at which he became intoxicated, beheaded him with his own sword. Liss shows the moment after the decapitation, when Judith is placing the severed head in a sack held up by her black servant. She grasps it by a tuft of hair but Holofernes's right eye can just be glimpsed beneath her arm, and blood gushes from the severed neck. The picture was probably painted in Rome, and its dramatic composition, theatrical contrasts of light and shade and gruesome detail clearly owe something to the example of the Italian painter Caravaggio, whose work was well known in the city.

Julius Schnorr von Carolsfeld, *Ruth in Boaz's Field*

1828, oil on canvas, 59 x 70 cm

Julius Schnorr von Carolsfeld was a leading artist in the group of German and Austrian painters known as the Nazarenes, who sought to purify German sacred art by reviving the principles and practices of art from the Middle Ages and Renaissance. He spent a decade in Italy, and something of the gentle light of the south can be detected in this work, which illustrates an Old Testament subject. The Moabite widow Ruth is gathering corn after the harvest to support her mother-in-law; she is greeted by the landowner Boaz, who eventually took pity on her straitened circumstances and married her. The Bible describes Ruth and Boaz as the grandparents of King David and the ancestors of Christ.

MYTHICAL WORLDS

During the Renaissance the colourful myths and legends of the classical world came to the fore as subjects in Italian art. Encounters with the art of Italy, and the new humanist learning based on a study of Greek and Roman texts, had a profound effect on artists in northern Europe. At a time when religious imagery was being questioned, pagan subjects may have offered patrons an appealing alternative, as well as a chance to demonstrate their erudition and refinement of taste. Cranach's patron, Frederick the Wise, Duke of Saxony, was known to favour mythological subjects. Cranach decorated Frederick's marriage bed with scenes from classical mythology and history, and although his large decorative schemes have been lost, many of his surviving panel paintings depict elegant female nudes such as the pagan goddesses Venus and Diana or the Roman noblewoman Lucretia.

The new rationalism promoted by humanist learning did not, however, preclude a fascination with the occult. Hans Baldung, who was trained by Dürer but set up his workshop in the city of Strasbourg, was obsessed by the theme of witches and produced a number of compositions in which they feature. The Holy Roman Emperor Rudolf II (1552–1612), a great connoisseur and collector who had come into direct contact with Italian art, was also drawn towards the esoteric and pagan, as well as complex allegories in which abstract ideas were given visual form. From around 1583, when he established his residence in Prague, he called into his service artists, alchemists, astronomers, philosophers and other humanists to make the city into 'a Parnassus of the arts'. In pursuit of this vision he commissioned several learned allegorical and mythological subjects from his court painters Bartholomeus Spranger and Hans von Aachen, who picked up and developed the attenuated Italian Mannerist style. The German painters of the following generation who went to Italy, such as Johann Liss, also produced a number of mythological works but in a style that bore more resemblance to the realism of Caravaggio. A similar blend of traditions from north and south of the Alps can be seen in eighteenth-century mythological and allegorical works, particularly the frescoes produced in southern Germany and Austria.

Hans Schäufelein, *The Rape of Europa*

about 1506–7, pen and black ink, 20 x 16.1 cm, The British Museum, London

A story told by the Roman poet Ovid provides the narrative for this animated drawing by Hans Schäufelein, who began his career by assisting Dürer. The princess Europa is abducted by the god Jupiter, who disguises himself as a beautiful white bull, encourages her to climb on his back, and carries her across the sea to the continent that will bear her name. Unlike in later depictions of the subject, the bull seems to be striding at a leisurely pace through the water, and Europa has been careful to draw up her feet and dress so they will not get wet.

Hans Baldung Grien, *Witches Sabbath*

1510, colour woodcut printed from two blocks, 37.5 x 25.7 cm

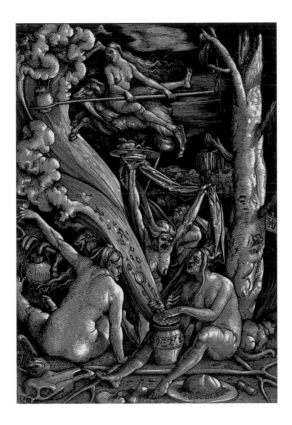

Baldung depicts four naked sorceresses stirring their cauldron in a forest setting while another flies about the sky above them on a goat. The print reflects fears about religious heresy and female sexuality, and it is hardly a coincidence that Baldung worked in Strasbourg, the city that in 1487 had published the *Malleus Maleficarum* (The Hammer of Witches), a handbook for rooting out witchcraft. Baldung used the new technique of colour woodblock to add tone to his composition and to suggest the frightening depths of an enchanted wood.

Lucas Cranach the Elder, *Cupid Complaining to Venus*

1526–7, oil on panel, 82.1 x 55.8 cm

Cranach's painting illustrates *The Honeycomb Stealer*, a poem by the Greek poet Theocritus, in which Cupid complains to Venus about being stung by bees after he has stolen a honeycomb. He asks how such a small creature could give him such a large wound. Venus, laughing, tells him that the effect is very similar to the wounds of love Cupid inflicts with his arrows. A Latin inscription in the upper right-hand corner underlines the moral: 'Young Cupid was stealing honey from a hive when a bee stung the thief on the finger. So it is for us: the brief and fleeting pleasure we seek/ comes mixed with wretched pain to do us harm.' This is one of the most elaborate of Cranach's many versions of the subject. The amusing anecdote is beautifully combined with the elegant nude in her decorative hat, the beauty of the beasts lurking in the forest and the distant vistas.

Lucas Cranach the Elder, *Primitive People*

1527–30, oil on oak, 51.5 x 35.8 cm

In this puzzling scene three naked women and babies and four fighting men are set against a grassy clearing in a forest, beyond which can be glimpsed rocky crags and a castle. Two of the women seem curiously disengaged from the pairs of fighting men, but the one on the left stares open-mouthed at the carnage and holds a sharpened stick with which to defend herself. The subject may have been inspired by contemporary derivations of classical texts by Hesiod and Ovid, which give accounts of the early development of the human race, following a decline from the harmonious Golden Age into the more warlike subsequent Ages of Silver, Bronze and Iron. It has been suggested that this picture represents the quarrelsome end to the Silver Age, but it also relates to the popular theme of 'Wild People' who lived in the forest, seen in other paintings by Cranach as well as those by Altdorfer and Dürer. Such pictures may have fascinated the hunting-obsessed Saxon courtiers as well as German humanists who were interested in the idea of the German forest and the origins of the primitive German people.

Hans von Aachen, *The Amazement of the Gods (?)*

probably 1590s, oil on copper, 35.5 x 45.8 cm

Most of the figures in this assembly are classical gods who can be identified by their attributes. Presiding over the composition are the embracing figures of Jupiter and his daughter Minerva. On the left are Diana, with her quiver and crescent moon headdress, and Mercury with his caduceus. Hercules wielding his club stands in the background while Neptune sits on the ground. In the right foreground Apollo stares in astonishment at the naked figure of Venus. A clue as to the picture's meaning is provided by a contemporary drawing by the artist with a similar composition, which is described as 'Jupiter abandons Venus and loves Minerva, with the amazement of all other pagan gods.' It was probably painted for the Emperor Rudolf II of Prague, who had a taste for erotic themes and learned allegories.

Johann Liss, *The Fall of Phaeton*

about 1624, oil on canvas, 126.5 x 110.3 cm

Book II of Ovid's *Metamorphoses* describes how when the sun god Phoebus allowed his son Phaeton to drive his chariot he was unable to keep control of the horses, who breathed fire, and veered too close to the earth, scorching the land and drying up rivers while setting cities and forests ablaze. Jupiter put a stop to the destruction by hurling a thunderbolt at the chariot, smashing it to pieces. Liss shows Phaeton hurtling from the skies to his death, while his sisters on the right and other nymphs on the left gaze up in dismay. The artist probably produced this canvas while he was living in Italy; its dramatic composition featuring fleshy nudes in expressive poses reflects the influence of both Flemish and Italian Baroque art, while the countryside around Rome provides the landscape setting.

Franz Anton Maulbertsch,
Allegory of the Continent of Asia

about 1750, oil on canvas, 43 x 48 cm

One of the most prominent German
Rococo painters, Maulbertsch
followed in the footsteps of the
Italian artist Giambattista Tiepolo,
who worked in southern Germany.
He is best remembered for his
frescoes and altarpieces, but also
painted small independent paintings such as this, which may have
been one of a suite of oil sketches
showing the four continents.
(The four continents were famously
depicted in Tiepolo's ceiling at
Würzburg, Bavaria, in 1753.) The
subject is the Orient, indicated by
the banner with a golden crescent
held by the woman in a white tur-
ban, which points towards a golden
star in the sky (the crescent and
star being symbols of the Ottoman
empire). On the left are figures with
a camel while on the right coffee is
poured by a crouching man, who
may be a captive.

THE NATURAL WORLD

Even before the sixteenth century, when painters began to think of landscape as an important subject in its own right, they were including it in the backgrounds to portraits and devotional works. Scenes of Adam and Eve in the Garden of Eden offered a natural opportunity to depict an earthly paradise, even if it was an entirely imaginary one, as did paintings of the Virgin Mary in a garden filled with flowers. In manuscripts there was a long-established tradition of representing the rural activities associated with different times of year in Books of Hours. This bucolic imagery spilled over into paintings depicting the months and seasons.

During the Renaissance, German artists began to focus more on the specific details of the countryside around them. There was a marked increase in the practice of making careful studies from nature to use as reference for paintings and prints. Some of the most celebrated examples are Dürer's meticulous drawings and watercolours of the landscapes he encountered as he travelled over the Alps, and his close-up views of plants and animals, in which every hair, leaf and blade of grass is lovingly recorded. But despite this almost scientific observation, plants and animals were frequently deployed for symbolic ends in paintings. Weeds, for example, might be shown in the foregrounds of Crucifixion scenes to suggest Christ's suffering, while specific flowers could indicate the individual virtues of the Virgin Mary.

Dürer's contemporaries, the artists of the Danube School, who drew their inspiration from the scenery around Regensburg, produced nature drawings as finished objects. But in their paintings precision took second place to expression and dramatic effect. Many of Cranach's works, particularly his panoramic hunting scenes, reveal a lively interest in landscape, but Altdorfer was the first artist to make landscape the main or only subject of a composition, sometimes leaving out signs of human presence altogether. Even in his compositions where figures are present, they are often dominated by mountains, burgeoning vegetation, pine forests and lowering skies.

Danube School paintings were rooted in the Gothic imagery and sensibility of northern Europe. The later generation of Romantic artists, particularly Friedrich, were also drawn to a specifically German landscape, which he saw as a divine creation that presented an antidote to civilisation. But for many nineteenth-century painters there was also poetry in townscape, where nature had been tamed by man.

Workshop of the Master of the Life of the Virgin, *The Conversion of Saint Hubert*

probably 1485–9, oil on oak, 123 x 83.2 cm

A dissolute courtier, Hubert (about 656–727) was converted to Christianity while out hunting during Holy Week, when a vision of a Crucifix appeared between the antlers of a stag he was about to shoot. The experience led him to follow a religious life, and he eventually became Bishop of Liège and was adopted as patron saint of hunters in the forest of Ardennes. The artist shows the conversion episode taking place in a forested setting, a path snaking away into the blue distance while the sky above glitters with the gold leaf commonly used for backgrounds of altarpieces. Hunters pursue their prey in the hills beyond as the splendidly dressed Hubert kneels before the stag. The artist has shown great skill in placing the shadows to convey the position of the figures in the foreground, even if the distant landscape resembles a backdrop.

Albrecht Dürer, *Saint Jerome*

about 1496, oil on pearwood, 23.1 x 17.4 cm

 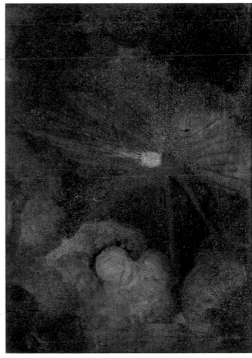

Saint Jerome (about 345–420) kneels before a rough-hewn Crucifix stuck in a tree trunk. He beats his breast in penitence, but it is the craggy landscape and turbulent sky that set the overall mood of the little panel. Dürer probably painted it soon after he had returned from his first journey to Italy, and the background resembles some of his Alpine landscapes rather than the Syrian desert where Jerome actually lived. In the foreground are a goldfinch and a bullfinch, both symbolic of Christ's Passion because of the patches of red in their plumage. On the reverse of the panel a glowing yellow oval emitting scarlet streaks of light breaks through a mass of swirling grey clouds. It is probably a symbolic reference to the tradition that Saint Jerome was a harbinger of Judgement Day rather than a depiction of an observed natural phenomenon.

89

Albrecht Dürer, *Irises*

about 1503, watercolour on paper, 77.5 x 31.3 cm,
Kunsthalle Bremen Kupferstichkabinett

'The more exactly one equals nature', wrote Dürer, 'the
better the picture looks.' The artist collected studies of
nature by others and made several himself, employing
his drawings and watercolours of plants, animals and
scenery to create a basis for his pictures. This striking
botanical study of an iris must have been used as
reference for the painting of the Virgin and Child that
was produced in his workshop.

Workshop of Albrecht Dürer, *Virgin and Child* (*'The Madonna with the Iris'*)

about 1500–10, oil on lime, 149.2 x 117.2 cm

The garden that surrounds the Virgin is rich with
symbolism. The flowering plants, all grown in northern
Europe, suggest that it is the month of May, and many
of them are specifically linked with her. The sword-like
leaves of the iris behind her head are reminders of the
swords that represent her sorrow. The peony on the far
right is known as the rose without thorns, like Mary
herself. The vine refers to Christ's future sacrifice because
of the association of his blood and Communion wine,
while the two butterflies may foretell his resurrection.
Dürer created a number of drawings and engravings of
the Virgin and Child in a garden, and his studies of plants
clearly provided the patterns for those shown here. But
this painting is thought to have been the work of one
or more of his assistants, who perhaps finished a
composition he had begun.

Albrecht Altdorfer, *Landscape with a Footbridge*

about 1518–20, oil on vellum on wood, 41.2 x 35.5 cm

Albrecht Altdorfer spent most of his life in the city of Regensburg in southern Germany. His work ranged from painted altarpieces to prints and landscape drawings and architecture. He probably travelled along the Danube on more than one occasion, and this painting – with its wooden bridge, distant church spire, and mountains – may have been inspired by the landscape of the river valley, although it probably does not show a specific place. Altdorfer was one of the first artists in Western Europe to show an interest in pure landscape, and in this panel he conveys the power and poetry of nature without reference to any human figure or narrative.

Albrecht Altdorfer, *Christ taking Leave of his Mother*

probably 1520, oil on lime, 141 x 111 cm

Christ has just told his mother Mary that he is leaving for Jerusalem. Knowing that this journey will lead to his death, she has collapsed with grief, and is supported by one of the four holy women who will later attend the entombment. Christ blesses her with his right hand while his left reaches out to reassure Saint John the Evangelist. Saint Peter holds his hands in a position of prayer. The landscape amplifies the picture's message: the trees behind Christ and the two apostles are flourishing while stark branches are outlined against a moody sky behind the sorrowing women. Christ's future suffering is hinted at in the menacing red clouds glimpsed through the ruined Gothic arch.

Hans Wertinger, *Summer*

about 1525, oil on wood, 23.2 x 39.5 cm

Like his contemporaries Altdorfer and
Cranach, Hans Wertinger painted
landscapes imbued with a strong sense of
atmosphere, although the sunny optimism
of this scene, with its emphasis on
productive labour and pleasure, presents a
marked contrast with the darker mood of
Altdorfer's *Landscape with a Footbridge*
(p. 102). It is probably one of a series of
paintings showing activities associated with
the four seasons. The gilded arch indicates
that it was part of a decorative scheme set
into wall panels, and the abruptly cropped
figure of the man and a cart on the right
would presumably have been continued in
the next scene in a frieze. Men harvest, fish,
hunt with falcons and shear sheep, while a
woman carries a basket of fruit on her head.
The background, showing a village on the
banks of a river or lake, is reminiscent of
the Bavarian countryside where Wertinger
lived.

Adam Elsheimer, *Saint Paul on Malta*

about 1600, oil on copper, 16.8 x 21.3 cm

The Bible records that Saint Paul and his companions were shipwrecked in Malta while on their way to Rome as prisoners, and were welcomed by the inhabitants. When they lit a fire to dry themselves, a viper appeared and bit Paul on the hand. He shook it off and suffered no harm, which led the islanders to assume that he was a god. Through the gloom it is just possible to see the encounter with the snake taking place on the left of the picture. According to the biblical account the event happened during the day, but Elsheimer has chosen to show it as a nocturnal scene. This certainly adds to the drama of the composition, the glowing fires and breaks in the clouds providing gleams of light in the prevailing darkness and highlighting the survivors and the waves on the stormy sea.

Caspar David Friedrich, *Winter Landscape*

probably 1811, oil on canvas, 32.5 x 45 cm

By the beginning of the 19th century, nature was increasingly seen by some artists as a powerful force capable of conveying human feelings and providing a connection with spiritual worlds. For certain painters, including Caspar David Friedrich, God's creation was a religious act and nature could reveal the divine. There is certainly an atmosphere of transcendence in this snow scene, in which a drama about salvation through Christian faith is being played out. A crippled man in the foreground has thrown away his crutches, and sits against a rock, his hands joined in prayer before a Crucifix. Both the rocks and the fir trees can be seen as symbols of faith, while the Gothic cathedral looming through the mist embodies a promise of life after death.

Eduard Gaertner, *The Friedrichsgracht, Berlin*

probably 1830s, oil on paper laid down on millboard, 25.5 x 44.6 cm

The only hint of nature in this cityscape is given in the trees on the left, which suggest an urban garden. The architectural painter Eduard Gaertner is remembered for the detailed views he painted of his native Berlin, which reflect the general public interest in a city that was being rebuilt after the Napoleonic wars; the Friedrichsgracht was a canal that ran through its centre. Gaertner's minutely rendered panoramas are bathed in summer light, their precise style presenting a contrast with the more painterly manner adopted by the next generation of artists.

Adolph Menzel, *Afternoon in the Tuileries Gardens*

1867, oil on canvas, 49 x 70 cm

In his bustling scene of the Tuileries Gardens in Paris Adolph Menzel tackled the type of subject favoured by the French Impressionists – urban landscapes in which well-to-do city dwellers enjoy their leisure. He painted the canvas following a visit to Paris in 1867, and it was probably inspired by Manet's *Music in the Tuileries Gardens* of 1862, now also in the National Gallery. Menzel even quotes from the picture: the figure of the man in a top hat, just to the right of the centre, resembles the figure of Manet's brother Eugène. However, Menzel's composition is more traditional than Manet's; it includes greater detail and is less broad in its handling. The effect of dappled sunlight falling through trees lends an immediacy and freshness to the picture, though it was painted in Berlin from memory and from sketches, far from the scene depicted.